RHAPSODY ON RUSSIAN FOLK SONGS

for concert band

JERRY H. BILIK

SYMPHONIC BAND SET
(WITH CONDUCTOR'S CONDENSED SCORE)

CONDUCTOR'S CONDENSED SCORE

EXTRA PARTS

SOUTHERN MUSIC PUBLISHING CO. INC.

PEER MUSIKVERLAG G.M.B.H.

SYMPHONIC SET

Piccolo	(4) 1st B♭ Cornet
(4) 1st Flute	(4) 2nd B♭ Cornet
(4) 2nd Flute	(4) 3rd B♭ Cornet
(2) Oboe	(2) 1st & 2nd B♭ Trumpets
English Horn	
(2) 1st & 2nd Bassoons	(2) 1st & 2nd F Horns
	(2) 3rd & 4th F Horns
E♭ Clarinet	
(4) 1st B♭ Clarinet	(2) 1st Trombone
(4) 2nd B♭ Clarinet	(2) 2nd Trombone
(4) 3rd B♭ Clarinet	(2) 3rd Trombone
Alto Clarinet	
Bass Clarinet	(2) Baritone (B.C.)
E♭ Contrabass Clarinet (optional)	Baritone (T.C.)
B♭ Contrabass Clarinet (optional)	
	(6) Basses
(2) 1st E♭ Alto Saxophone	String Bass
(2) 2nd E♭ Alto Saxophone	
Tenor Saxophone	Timpani
Baritone Saxophone	(4) Percussion

CONDUCTOR'S CONDENSED SCORE

PROGRAM NOTES

The RHAPSODY ON RUSSIAN FOLK SONGS was composed originally for the University of Michigan Symphony Band's tour of the Soviet Union in 1961. It was felt that a piece employing popular Russian folksongs, arranged, conducted, and performed by American musicians, would serve to illustrate the universality of music to the Russian audiences. That this aim succeeded is attested to by the fact that the audience response was so enthusiastic at the premiere performance, in Kiev, it was necessary for Dr. William D. Revelli, Director of the Michigan Band, to repeat the entire work before continuing his program.

The songs used were taken directly from Russian manuscripts especially prepared and sent to the University from the Ministry of Culture in Moscow. As listed in the score, they are:

" NIGHT "

" SPARROW HILLS "

" OH, YOU SNOW—DROP TREE "

" AH, THERE IS MORE THAN ONE PATH THRU THE FIELD "

" THE BIRCH TREE "

To allow the director to shorten, or simplify the work, several optional cuts have been provided.

Duration: 6½ minutes

Grade: medium

RHAPSODY ON RUSSIAN FOLK SONGS

Conductor

JERRY H. BILIK

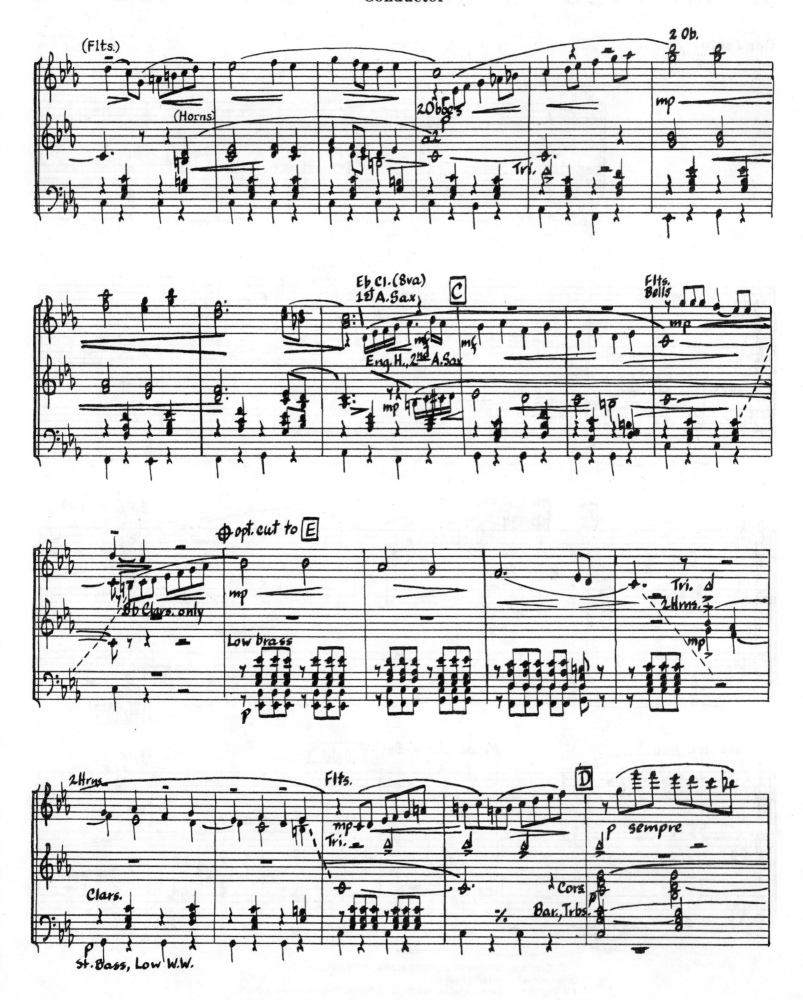

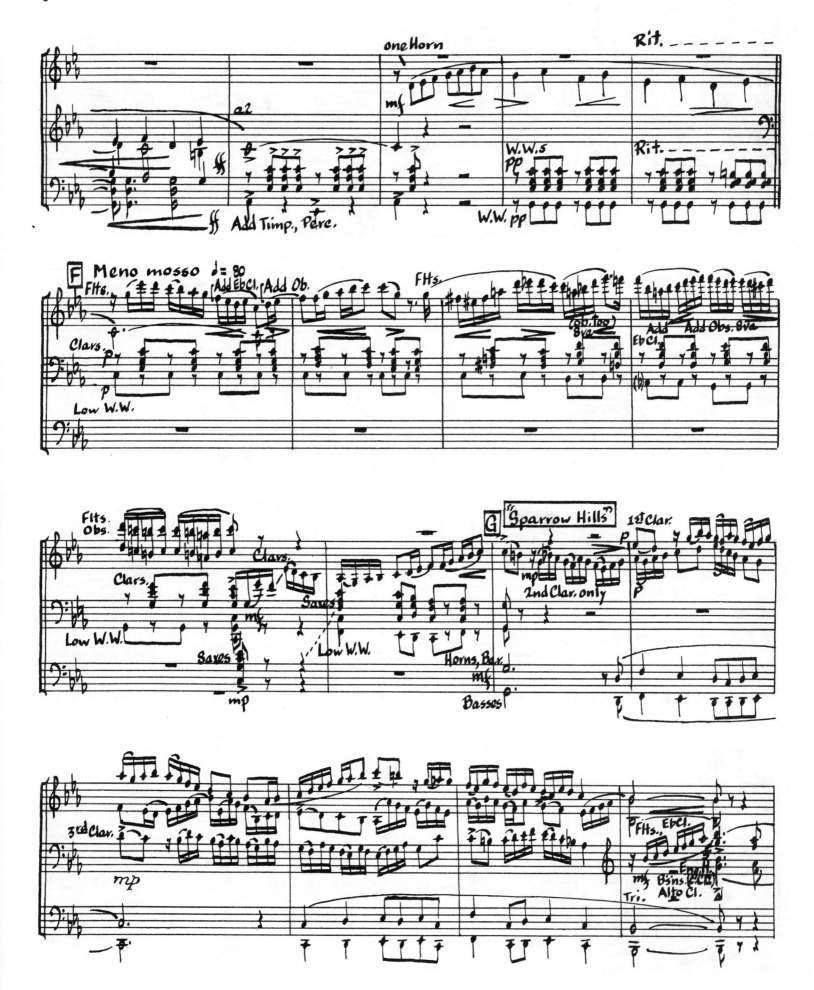

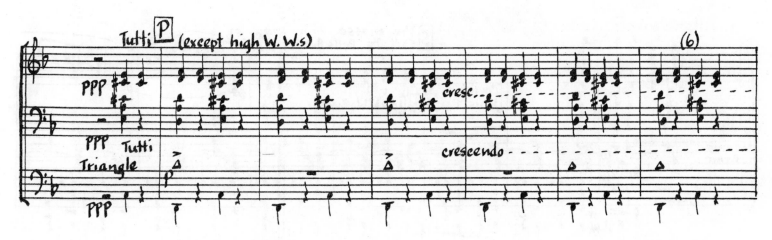

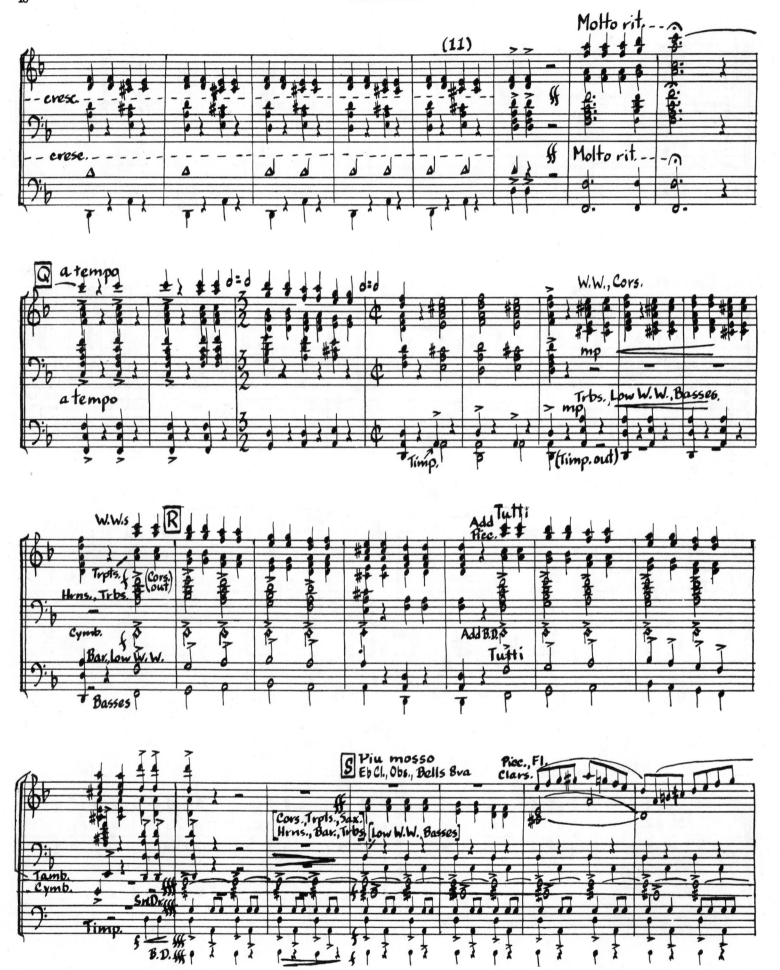

Conductor

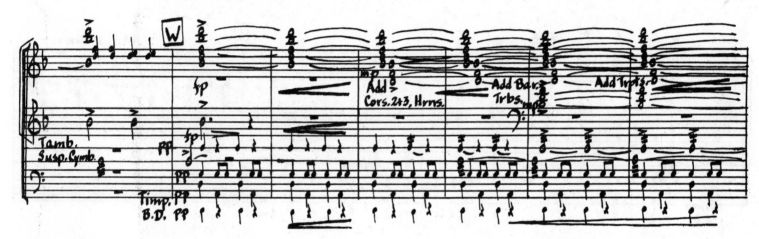

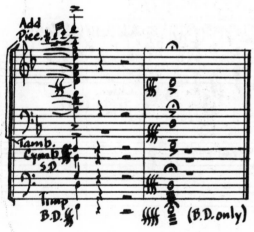

RHAPSODY ON RUSSIAN FOLK SONGS

1st Flute
Piccolo

JERRY H. BILIK

1st Flute
Piccolo

RHAPSODY ON RUSSIAN FOLK SONGS

1st Flute
Piccolo

JERRY H. BILIK

RHAPSODY ON RUSSIAN FOLK SONGS

1st Flute
Piccolo

JERRY H. BILIK

1st Flute
Piccolo

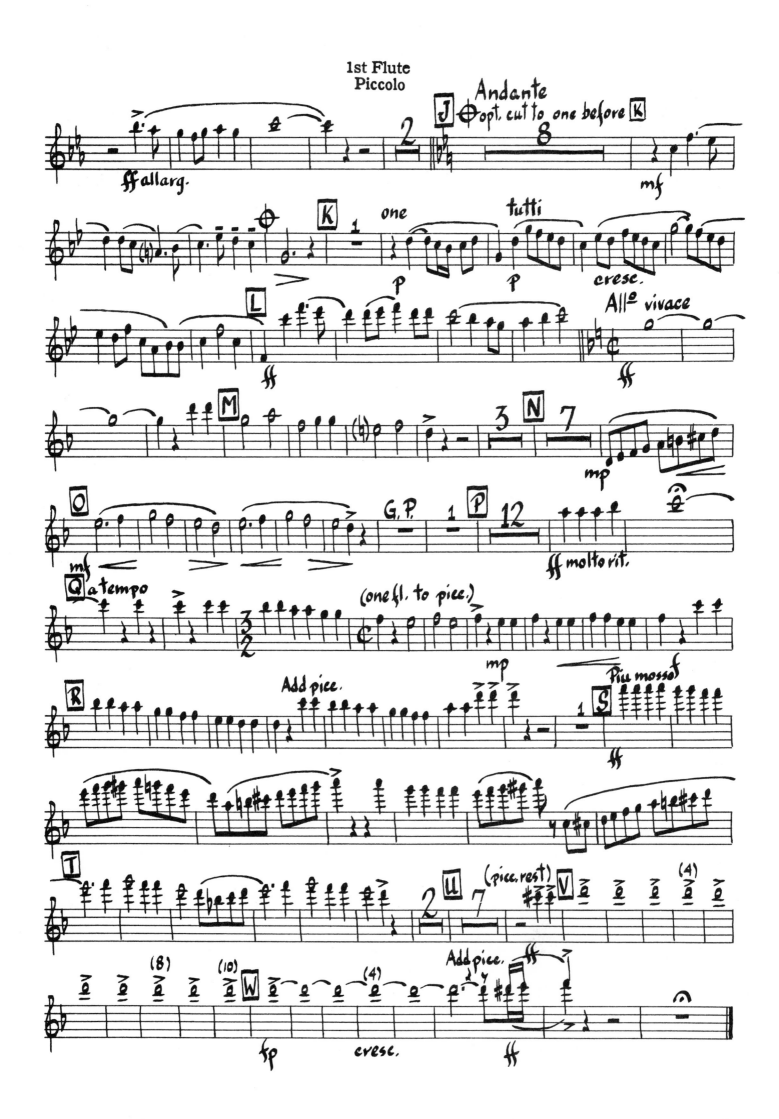

RHAPSODY ON RUSSIAN FOLK SONGS

1st Flute
Piccolo

JERRY H. BILIK

1st Flute
Piccolo

RHAPSODY ON RUSSIAN FOLK SONGS

1st Flute
Piccolo

JERRY H. BILIK

1st Flute
Piccolo

RHAPSODY ON RUSSIAN FOLK SONGS

2nd Flute

JERRY H. BILIK

2nd Flute

RHAPSODY ON RUSSIAN FOLK SONGS

2nd Flute

JERRY H. BILIK

2nd Flute

RHAPSODY ON RUSSIAN FOLK SONGS

2nd Flute

Jerry H. Bilik

2nd Flute

RHAPSODY ON RUSSIAN FOLK SONGS

2nd Flute

Jerry H. Bilik

2nd Flute

RHAPSODY ON RUSSIAN FOLK SONGS

Oboes

JERRY H. BILIK

Oboes

RHAPSODY ON RUSSIAN FOLK SONGS

Oboes

JERRY H. BILIK

Oboes

RHAPSODY ON RUSSIAN FOLK SONGS

English Horn

JERRY H. BILIK

English Horn

RHAPSODY ON RUSSIAN FOLK SONGS

1st & 2nd **Bassoons**

JERRY H. BILIK

1st & 2nd **Bassoons**

RHAPSODY ON RUSSIAN FOLK SONGS

1st & 2nd **Bassoons**

JERRY H. BILIK

1st & 2nd **Bassoons**

RHAPSODY ON RUSSIAN FOLK SONGS

Eb Clarinet

JERRY H. BILIK

Eb Clarinet

RHAPSODY ON RUSSIAN FOLK SONGS

1st Bb Clarinet

JERRY H. BILIK

1st B♭ Clarinet

RHAPSODY ON RUSSIAN FOLK SONGS

1st Bb Clarinet

JERRY H. BILIK

1st B♭ Clarinet

RHAPSODY ON RUSSIAN FOLK SONGS

1st B♭ Clarinet

JERRY H. BILIK

1st B♭ Clarinet

RHAPSODY ON RUSSIAN FOLK SONGS

1st B♭ Clarinet

JERRY H. BILIK

1st Bb Clarinet

RHAPSODY ON RUSSIAN FOLK SONGS

2nd Bb Clarinet

Jerry H. Bilik

2nd B♭ Clarinet

RHAPSODY ON RUSSIAN FOLK SONGS

2nd Bb Clarinet

JERRY H. BILIK

2nd B♭ Clarinet

RHAPSODY ON RUSSIAN FOLK SONGS

2nd Bb Clarinet

JERRY H. BILIK

2nd Bb Clarinet

RHAPSODY ON RUSSIAN FOLK SONGS

2nd Bb Clarinet

JERRY H. BILIK

2nd B♭ Clarinet

RHAPSODY ON RUSSIAN FOLK SONGS

3rd B♭ Clarinet

JERRY H. BILIK

3rd B♭ Clarinet

RHAPSODY ON RUSSIAN FOLK SONGS

3rd Bb Clarinet

JERRY H. BILIK

3rd B♭ Clarinet

RHAPSODY ON RUSSIAN FOLK SONGS

3rd Bb Clarinet

JERRY H. BILIK

3rd B♭ Clarinet

RHAPSODY ON RUSSIAN FOLK SONGS

3rd Bb Clarinet

JERRY H. BILIK

3rd B♭ Clarinet

RHAPSODY ON RUSSIAN FOLK SONGS

Alto Clarinet

JERRY H. BILIK

Alto Clarinet

RHAPSODY ON RUSSIAN FOLK SONGS

Bass Clarinet

JERRY H. BILIK

Bass Clarinet

RHAPSODY ON RUSSIAN FOLK SONGS

Eb Contrabass Clarinet

JERRY H. BILIK

Eb Contrabass Clarinet

RHAPSODY ON RUSSIAN FOLK SONGS

Bb Contrabass Clarinet

Jerry H. BILIK

Bb Contrabass Clarinet

RHAPSODY ON RUSSIAN FOLK SONGS

1st E♭ Alto Saxophone

JERRY H. BILIK

1st E♭ Alto Saxophone

RHAPSODY ON RUSSIAN FOLK SONGS

1st E♭ Alto Saxophone

JERRY H. BILIK

1st E♭ Alto Saxophone

RHAPSODY ON RUSSIAN FOLK SONGS

2nd Eb Alto Saxophone

Jerry H. Bilik

2nd E♭ Alto Saxophone

RHAPSODY ON RUSSIAN FOLK SONGS

2nd E♭ Alto Saxophone

JERRY H. BILIK

2nd E♭ Alto Saxophone

RHAPSODY ON RUSSIAN FOLK SONGS

Tenor Saxophone

Jerry H. Bilik

Tenor Saxophone

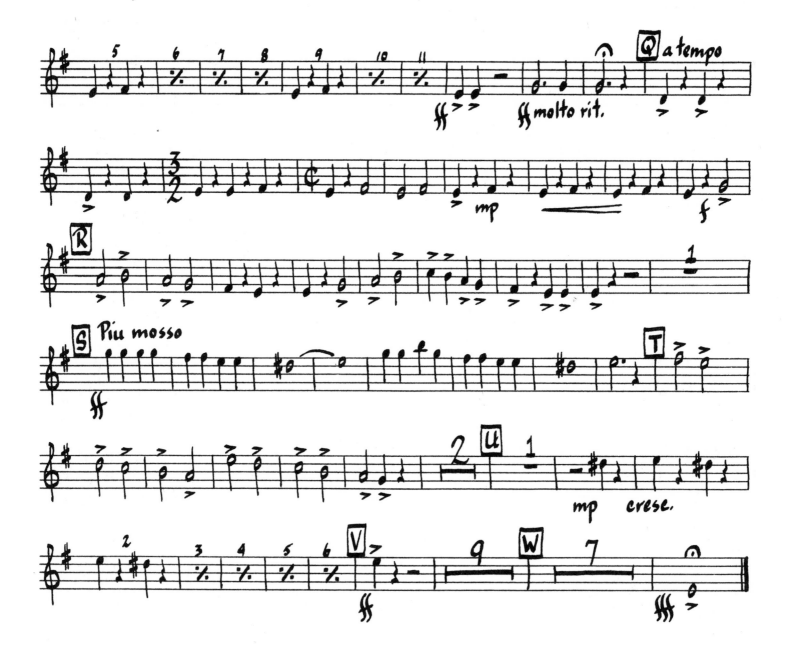

RHAPSODY ON RUSSIAN FOLK SONGS

Baritone Saxophone

JERRY H. BILIK

Baritone Saxophone

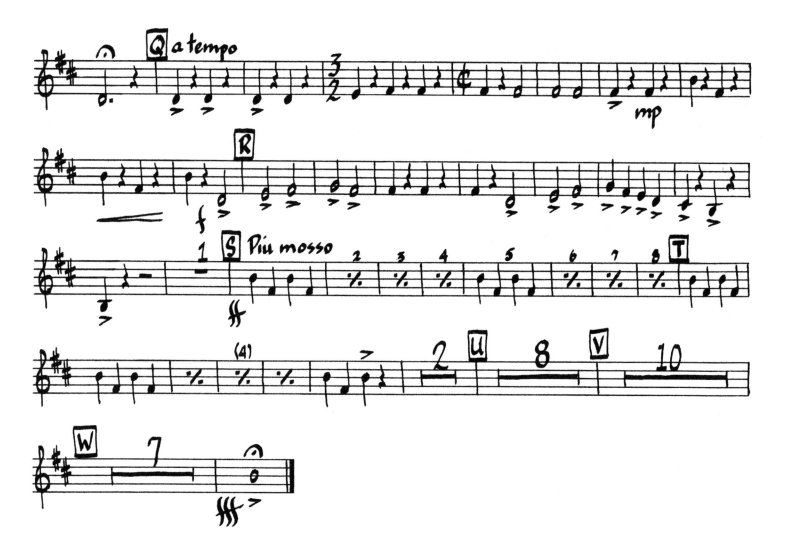

RHAPSODY ON RUSSIAN FOLK SONGS

1st Bb Cornet

JERRY H. BILIK

1st Bb Cornet

RHAPSODY ON RUSSIAN FOLK SONGS

1st Bb Cornet

JERRY H. BILIK

1st Bb Cornet

RHAPSODY ON RUSSIAN FOLK SONGS

1st Bb Cornet

JERRY H. BILIK

RHAPSODY ON RUSSIAN FOLK SONGS

1st Bb Cornet

JERRY H. BILIK

1st Bb Cornet

RHAPSODY ON RUSSIAN FOLK SONGS

2nd Bb Cornet

JERRY H. BILIK

2nd Bb Cornet

RHAPSODY ON RUSSIAN FOLK SONGS

2nd Bb Cornet

JERRY H. BILIK

2nd Bb Cornet

RHAPSODY ON RUSSIAN FOLK SONGS

2nd Bb Cornet

JERRY H. BILIK

2nd B♭ Cornet

RHAPSODY ON RUSSIAN FOLK SONGS

2nd Bb Cornet

JERRY H. BILIK

2nd B♭ Cornet

RHAPSODY ON RUSSIAN FOLK SONGS

3rd Bb Cornet

JERRY H. BILIK

3rd Bb Cornet

RHAPSODY ON RUSSIAN FOLK SONGS

3rd Bb Cornet

JERRY H. BILIK

3rd Bb Cornet

RHAPSODY ON RUSSIAN FOLK SONGS

3rd Bb Cornet

JERRY H. BILIK

3rd B♭ Cornet

RHAPSODY ON RUSSIAN FOLK SONGS

3rd Bb Cornet

JERRY H. BILIK

3rd B♭ Cornet

RHAPSODY ON RUSSIAN FOLK SONGS

1st & 2nd **Trumpets**

JERRY H. BILIK

1st & 2nd Trumpets

RHAPSODY ON RUSSIAN FOLK SONGS

1st & 2nd **Trumpets**

JERRY H. BILIK

1st & 2nd **Trumpets**

RHAPSODY ON RUSSIAN FOLK SONGS

Jerry H. Bilik

1st & 2nd F Horns

RHAPSODY ON RUSSIAN FOLK SONGS

JERRY H. BILIK

1st & 2nd F Horns

1st & 2nd F Horns

RHAPSODY ON RUSSIAN FOLK SONGS

3rd & 4th F Horns

JERRY H. BILIK

3rd & 4th F Horns

RHAPSODY ON RUSSIAN FOLK SONGS

3rd & 4th F Horns

JERRY H. BILIK

RHAPSODY ON RUSSIAN FOLK SONGS

1st Trombone

JERRY H. BILIK

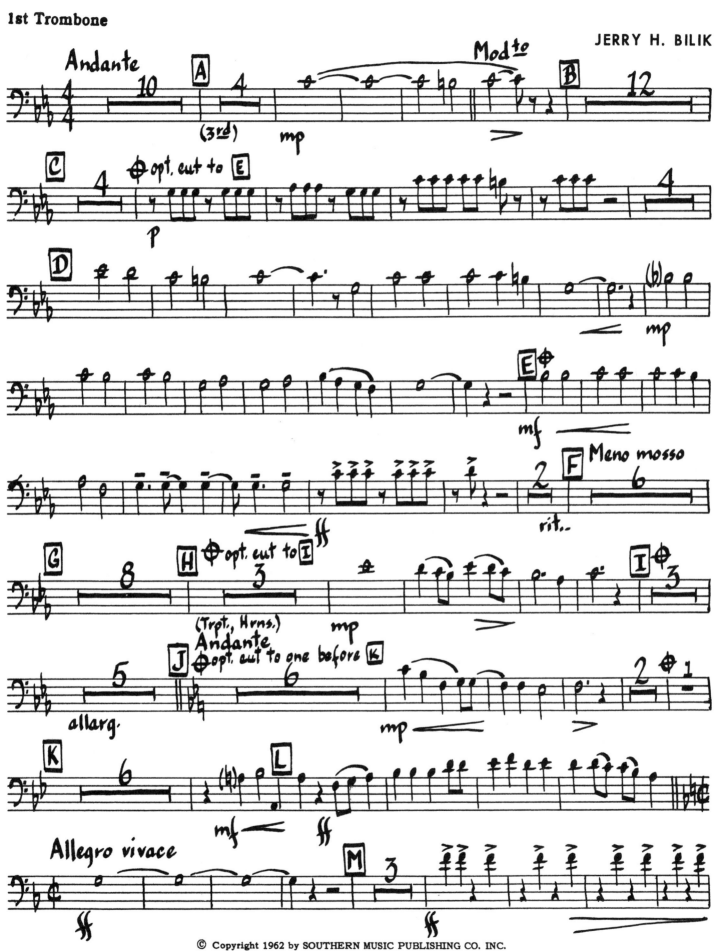

1st Trombone

RHAPSODY ON RUSSIAN FOLK SONGS

1st Trombone

JERRY H. BILIK

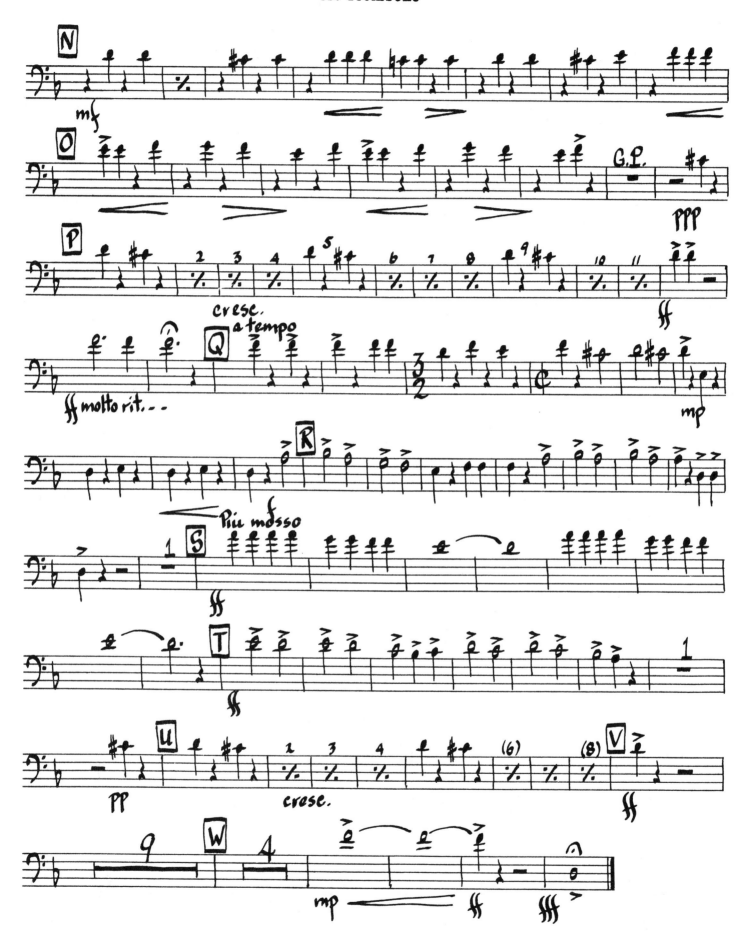

1st Trombone

RHAPSODY ON RUSSIAN FOLK SONGS

2nd Trombone

Jerry H. Bilik

2nd Trombone

RHAPSODY ON RUSSIAN FOLK SONGS

2nd Trombone

JERRY H. BILIK

2nd Trombone

RHAPSODY ON RUSSIAN FOLK SONGS

3rd Trombone

JERRY H. BILIK

3rd Trombone

RHAPSODY ON RUSSIAN FOLK SONGS

3rd Trombone

Jerry H. Bilik

3rd Trombone

RHAPSODY ON RUSSIAN FOLK SONGS

Baritone 𝄢

JERRY H. BILIK

Baritone 𝄢

RHAPSODY ON RUSSIAN FOLK SONGS

Baritone 𝄢:

JERRY H. BILIK

Baritone 𝄢

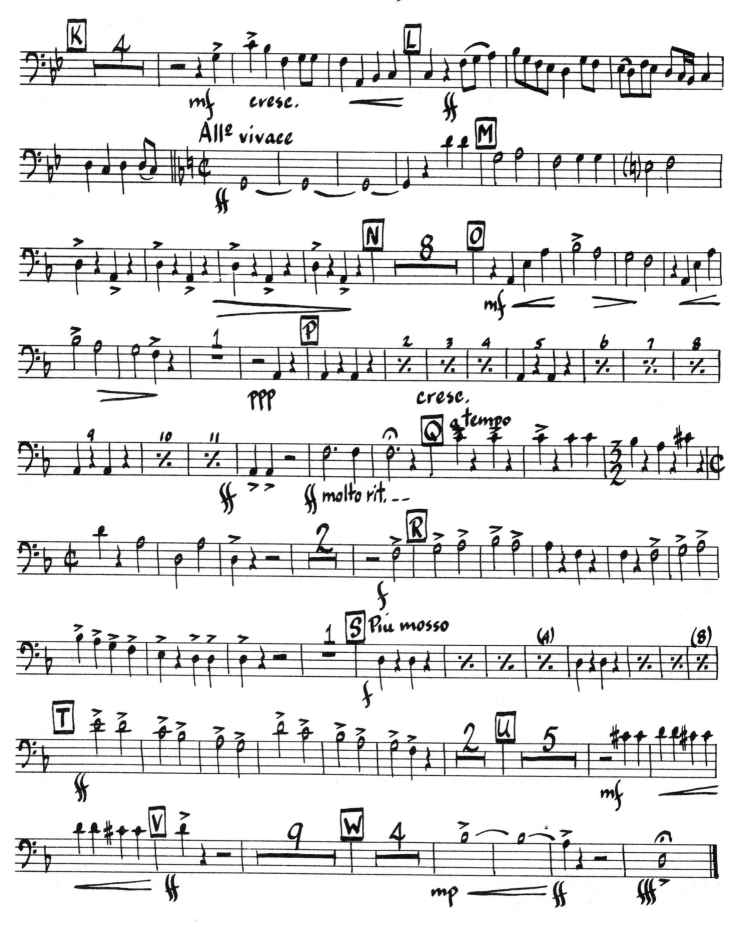

RHAPSODY ON RUSSIAN FOLK SONGS

Baritone

JERRY H. BILIK

Baritone

RHAPSODY ON RUSSIAN FOLK SONGS

Basses

Jerry H. Bilik

Basses

RHAPSODY ON RUSSIAN FOLK SONGS

Basses

JERRY H. BILIK

Basses

RHAPSODY ON RUSSIAN FOLK SONGS

Basses

JERRY H. BILIK

Basses

RHAPSODY ON RUSSIAN FOLK SONGS

Basses

JERRY H. BILIK

Basses

RHAPSODY ON RUSSIAN FOLK SONGS

Basses

Jerry H. Bilik

Basses

RHAPSODY ON RUSSIAN FOLK SONGS

Basses

JERRY H. BILIK

Basses

RHAPSODY ON RUSSIAN FOLK SONGS

String Bass

Jerry H. Bilik

String Bass

RHAPSODY ON RUSSIAN FOLK SONGS

Timpani

Jerry H. BILIK

RHAPSODY ON RUSSIAN FOLK SONGS

Percussion

JERRY H. BILIK

4

RHAPSODY ON RUSSIAN FOLK SONGS

Percussion

JERRY H. BILIK

RHAPSODY ON RUSSIAN FOLK SONGS

Percussion

JERRY H. BILIK

RHAPSODY ON RUSSIAN FOLK SONGS

Percussion

JERRY H. BILIK